TIGER WITH WINGS
The Great Horned Owl

by Barbara Juster Esbensen
illustrated by Mary Barrett Brown

ORCHARD BOOKS   NEW YORK

My thanks to the naturalists at the Minnesota Zoo. Steve Martin allowed me to experience the owl's silent flight, and Joanna Watson kindly gave me an up-close introduction to Hoot'n Annie, their resident great horned owl.

—B.J.E.

My deep appreciation to Ken Christensen of the Treasure Coast Audubon Wildlife Hospital, whose patience and help allowed me to follow Junior to adulthood.

Thank you also to the Vermont Institute of Natural Sciences—and Nancy Reed—for their cheerful assistance.

—M.B.B.

Orchard Books, 95 Madison Avenue, New York, NY 10016

Manufactured in the United States of America. Printed by Barton Press, Inc. Bound by Horowitz/Rae. Book design by Jean Krulis.

Hardcover   3   5   7   9   10   8   6   4   2
Paperback   1   3   5   7   9   10   8   6   4   2

The text of this book is set in 14 point Bembo. The illustrations are watercolor reproduced in full color.

Library of Congress Cataloging-in-Publication Data
Esbensen, Barbara Juster. Tiger with wings : the great horned owl / by Barbara Juster Esbensen ; illustrated by Mary Barrett Brown. p.   cm.   Summary: Describes the hunting technique, physical characteristics, mating ritual, and nesting and child-rearing practices of the great horned owl.   ISBN 0-531-05940-5 (tr.)
ISBN 0-531-08540-6 (lib.)   ISBN 0-531-07071-9 (pbk.)   1. Great horned owl—Juvenile literature.
[1. Great horned owl.   2. Owls.]   I. Brown, Mary Barrett, ill.   II. Title.
QL696.S83E73   1991   598'.97—dc20   90-23034

I gratefully dedicate this book to
Karen Klockner,
editor and dear friend.
Without her thoughtful caring,
no owl
would be flying across these pages.
—B.J.E.

With special love to
Sam, Kelly, Chip, and Mike,
who keep me ever alert
to the wonders of growing up.
—M.B.B.

The great horned owl is such a fierce hunter that it is often compared to a tiger. Like the tiger, the great horned owl hunts in the dark, and it kills instantly. Its stripes let it blend with the forest patterns of dim light and shadow. Its two-inch feather tufts look like a tiger's ears, and it has a face like an angry cat. It is a tiger with wings—a tiger that can fly almost unseen through the darkness.

Gliding in soundless flight, the great horned owl uses its eyes and its ears to find food. It will always return with something. It is an accurate hunter whose powerful silent dive means certain death for any unsuspecting prey.

Just before it strikes, the owl's head snaps back, its tail goes down, and its feet stretch forward to grab the kill. Each powerful foot has four toes. Each toe ends in a talon as sharp as a razor blade. The talon is curved like a pirate's cutlass—and it is as deadly. When the talons strike an animal, they spread wide apart and lock onto it.

The prey usually dies immediately. The owl uses its sharp, curved beak to tear larger food into small pieces, but it swallows small animals whole. It may carry its dinner, grasped in one powerful foot, to a perch on a limb. Owls never carry food in their beaks.

The great horned owl's wingspread is more than fifty inches. The wings and talons are so strong that it can carry a heavy animal, such as a skunk, to a branch as high as sixty feet above the ground. Skunks are one of this owl's most common meals. Although the great horned owl has an astounding sense of sight and hearing, its sense of smell is very weak. The odor of the skunk doesn't affect it at all.

The great horned owl will eat bats, flying squirrels, rabbits, woodchucks, mice, an occasional cat, and even another owl. It swallows everything: fur, bones, and claws. Later the owl coughs up the indigestible parts of its prey in little packages of bones and fur called pellets. Finding owl pellets on the ground is a sure sign an owl has a nest nearby.

In most species, the male birds have brighter feathers than the females and attract their mates with brilliant plumage. Many male birds are larger than their mates. But the plumage of male and female great horned owls is exactly the same, and the female is actually the larger one, often as tall as twenty-five inches. Both male and female have brown and rust and tan feathers. The colors form striped patterns over most of their large bodies and wide-spreading wings. Sketchy brown stripes decorate their breasts. Under their chins a feathery ruff forms a snowy neckpiece.

Early in winter the great horned owls of the northern forests begin to call. HOO-HOOOO-HOO-HOO! HOO-HOOOO-HOO-HOO! The cold, dark air echoes with their booming voices. They can shriek or wail or growl. Their voices can even sound like barking dogs.

Over and over the owls hoot at one another, and their mysterious sounds travel from one part of the forest to another. They will even hoot back at a person who walks through the forest at night hooting at them, under the winter sky. The sound grows louder each night as great horned owls begin to look for mates.

Most birds do not mate and raise their families until spring. Other owls look for nesting places and lay their eggs in late winter. But the great horned owls start their families earlier than any of their relatives. Their eggs are laid during the early days of February. In northern climates this means that the eggs are laid when the weather is snowy and freezing cold.

When a male owl finds a mate, he fluffs his feathers, spreads his wings, and bobs up and down on a branch in front of her. Then he launches himself off of his perch and shoots high into the night air. Tumbling and falling, he does a series of impressive air swoops and ground loops before returning to the branch. There, he hops and bows and turns around. He snaps his beak and jumps along the branch to his own rhythmic beat.

If this courtship dance attracts the female owl, she fluffs her feathers too, and joins her partner, hopping and bobbing along the limb, keeping time to the same silent rhythm. They snap their beaks at each other, making the clickety-clack sound of castanets under the winter stars. Then the two birds rub their heads and beaks together, face each other, and hoot together into the frosty night.

Great horned owls mate for life.

During courtship, the male often leaves the branch to find food for his mate. He spreads his enormous wings and floats off through the forest. His wide, rounded wings do not make a sound as they move through the cold air.

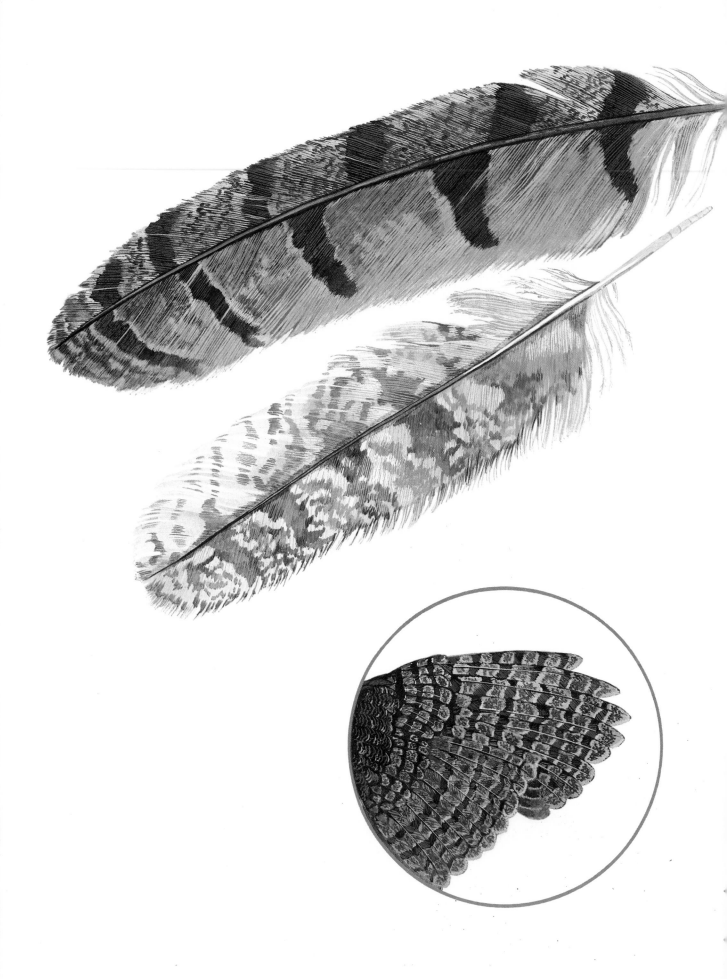

Owls that hunt at night have soft edges on their flight feathers. The feathers on the surface of their wings are like velvet. Owl bones are paper thin and filled with air, so these great wings give the owl a tremendous amount of lift. When the owl pumps its wings, the rushing air is trapped in the soft feathers, and the sound is muffled. These soft feathers cover the great horned owl's entire body. Even its legs and all four toes are covered with soundproofing velvet muffs.

The great horned owl must fly silently so that it can hear the slightest sound. If its own wings made any noise, it would not be able to locate its prey.

Although the feathery horns on the great horned owl's head look like ears, they are only feathers. The owl can raise and lower them. It will always raise them to show anger. The owl's real ears are long narrow holes on either side of its skull.

Scientists believe that great horned owls probably use their amazing sense of hearing even more than their sharp eyesight. The ear holes are nearly as long as the owl's head, and the eardrum is the largest of any bird's. Besides having an inner ear, owls are the only birds with an outer ear too—a small thin flap of skin that catches sound waves just the way human ears do. The ear flap is slightly higher on one side of the great horned owl's head than on the other side. This positioning lets sound into the ears from different directions.

The ear flap is hidden under the ruff of short, flattened feathers you can see around each big yellow eye. Those feathers are called the owl's facial disk. They give owls a "face" that looks almost human. The owl can move its facial disk back and forth a little. It may be that the circle of stiff feathers helps direct sound into the owl's ears.

Like its ears, the great horned owl's eyes are perfectly suited for life as a nighttime hunter. All owls can see in daylight, and a few owls fly and hunt during the day. But because the great horned owl's eyes are extremely sensitive to light, it hunts at night and sleeps during the day.

The great horned owl's eyes are one hundred times more acute than human eyes. They can be focused instantly to see either near or far. While human eyes have cone cells that allow us to see color and rod cells that gather light, the great horned owl's eyes have mostly rod cells. It has so few cone cells that it sees only in black and white. But the smallest amount of light from a few stars is enough to let this owl hunt at night.

Owls have an upper eyelid with lashes made of feathers; the owl can blink its eyes like a person can. No other bird has an upper eyelid. But all birds raise a bottom eyelid when they sleep, and great horned owls have this lid too. In addition they have a transparent third eyelid that flips across the owl's eyes from one side to the other like a windshield wiper. It acts as a safety covering when the owl is flying or when the light is suddenly too strong.

Like the eyes in a human face, both of the owl's eyes face forward, so that owls, like humans, have binocular vision. This means that owls see things as rounded shapes, not flat, and lets them judge distances very accurately. An owl's eyes are nearly the same size as a human's, but its head is much smaller, so the eyes seem enormous. For hundreds of years, owls were thought to be particularly wise—their staring, human appearance and nocturnal habits made people think they knew mysterious and important things. Actually, ravens, geese, and crows are much smarter than owls. The owl's brain is smaller than those two eyes together!

The owl's big eyes don't move from side to side the way human eyes do. To see something to the right or left, an owl must turn its head. People have seven neck bones, so a person can look no further than over each shoulder. The owl has fourteen very flexible neck bones. It can actually swivel its head to see what's directly behind it, while the rest of its body is still facing forward! Then the owl can whip its head to the front again so fast it looks almost as though it has revolved completely—like a spinning top.

Owls are not good nest builders. They always try to find something ready-made if they can. Great horned owls are usually birds of the trees. These birds are found, however, throughout the entire United States (except Hawaii) and Canada, so if they live in a treeless place, they will put together a straggly nest on the edge of a cliff, or on a pile of rocks above the desert floor. In the northern woods, the great horned owls often add some feathers, leaves, and sticks to a hole in a hollow tree. If they can find the roomy nest of another big bird, like an eagle or a hawk, they will take it over as their own.

Since it is wintertime, the builder of the nest has usually left for warmer climates. But if the builder returns, the great horned owl puffs up its feathers until it seems to be twice its normal size, while hissing and snapping its dangerous beak. Even eagles have been known to retreat after trying to reclaim a nest from a great horned owl.

Egg laying begins while snow is still falling, ice is still on the lakes, and the air is freezing cold. The mother owl pulls her softest feathers from the underside of her body and lines the nest with them. The part of her body where she has removed those feathers is called her brood patch.

Then she lays two, or sometimes three, round white eggs the size of jumbo chicken eggs, with a rough shell. The mother owl lays them two or three days apart. Her brood patch is very warm, and she keeps all the eggs safe under her body so that they will be able to hatch. Her mate brings her food so that she does not have to leave the nest and expose the eggs to the cold. Sitting there unmoving on the nest for four weeks in the falling snow, she may sometimes look like a big white statue of an owl.

The first-laid egg begins to hatch sometime during the fourth week. The other eggs hatch three or four days apart, so there are owlets of different ages and sizes in the nest at the same time. They are covered with tiny soft white feathers called down. This downy coat helps them stay warm, snuggled beneath the big wings and brood patch of their mother.

Baby owls are about the size of baby chicks, but they are not able to take care of themselves the way baby chicks or ducklings can. A baby chick can run about and scratch for food soon after hatching from the egg, and baby ducklings can swim soon after they hatch.

But owlets are helpless. They can't stand up; their big heads wobble on skinny necks; and their eyes do not open until they are ten days old. Even after their eyes are open, the owlets stay under their parents' wings for a month.

Great horned owls are always dangerous birds. But with babies in the nest, they are at their most ferocious. They will attack anything that comes near, clawing with sharp talons and deadly beak. Most animals and other large birds stay away from the nest of a great horned owl.

At nightfall, first one and then the other parent sails out in search of food for the babies. They may each make as many as a dozen trips back and forth with food for the ravenous owlets. The young owls stay in the nest until they are five weeks old, and they don't try to fly until they are ten weeks old.